DATE _____

Prayer

TODAY'S PASSAGE

PREACHER

NOTES
_____
_____
_____
_____
_____
_____
_____
_____
_____
_____
_____
_____

KEY VERSES

PRAYER
_____
_____
_____
_____
_____
_____

KEY POINTS

_____
_____
_____
_____
_____
_____
_____

APPLICATION

Prayer journal

DATE _____

| TODAY'S PASSAGE | PREACHER | SERMON TOPIC |

NOTES

_____

_____

_____

_____

_____

_____

_____

_____

_____

_____

_____

_____

KEY VERSES

PRAYER

_____

_____

_____

_____

_____

_____

_____

_____

_____

_____

_____

_____

_____

_____

_____

_____

KEY POINTS

APPLICATION

Prayer journal

DATE _____

TODAY'S PASSAGE | PREACHER | SERMON TOPIC

NOTES
_____
_____
_____
_____
_____
_____
_____
_____
_____
_____

KEY VERSES

PRAYER
_____
_____
_____
_____
_____
_____
_____
_____
_____
_____
_____
_____

KEY POINTS

APPLICATION

DATE _____

Prayer journal

NOTES
_____
_____
_____
_____
_____
_____
_____
_____
_____
_____
_____

KEY VERSES

PRAYER
_____
_____
_____
_____
_____
_____
_____

KEY POINTS

_____
_____
_____
_____
_____
_____
_____
_____
_____

APPLICATION

DATE _____

Prayer journal

    PREACHER   SERMON TOPIC

NOTES
_____
_____
_____
_____
_____
_____
_____
_____
_____
_____
_____

KEY VERSES

PRAYER
_____
_____
_____
_____
_____

KEY POINTS

_____
_____
_____
_____
_____
_____

APPLICATION

DATE _____

Prayer journal

TODAY'S PASSAGE   PREACHER   SERMON TOPIC

NOTES
_____
_____
_____
_____
_____
_____
_____
_____
_____
_____
_____
_____
_____

KEY VERSES

PRAYER
_____
_____
_____
_____
_____
_____
_____
_____
_____
_____
_____
_____
_____
_____
_____

KEY POINTS

APPLICATION

Prayer journal

DATE _____

TODAY'S PASSAGE   PREACHER   SERMON TOPIC

NOTES
_____
_____
_____
_____
_____
_____
_____
_____
_____
_____

KEY VERSES

PRAYER
_____
_____
_____
_____
_____

KEY POINTS

_____
_____
_____
_____
_____
_____
_____

APPLICATION

DATE _____

Prayer journal

| TODAY'S PASSAGE | PREACHER | SERMON TOPIC |

NOTES
_____
_____
_____
_____
_____
_____
_____
_____
_____
_____
_____

KEY VERSES

PRAYER
_____
_____
_____
_____
_____
_____
_____
_____
_____
_____
_____
_____
_____
_____

KEY POINTS

APPLICATION

DATE _____

Prayer journal

TODAY'S PASSAGE | PREACHER | SERMON TOPIC

NOTES

_____
_____
_____
_____
_____
_____
_____
_____
_____
_____
_____

KEY VERSES

PRAYER

_____
_____
_____
_____
_____
_____
_____
_____
_____
_____
_____
_____
_____

KEY POINTS

APPLICATION

DATE _____

Prayer journal

TODAY'S PASSAGE   PREACHER   SERMON TOPIC

NOTES
_____
_____
_____
_____
_____
_____
_____
_____
_____
_____
_____
_____

KEY VERSES

PRAYER
_____
_____
_____
_____
_____
_____
_____

KEY POINTS

_____
_____
_____
_____
_____
_____
_____
_____

APPLICATION

DATE _____

Prayer journal

TODAY'S PASSAGE | PREACHER | SERMON TOPIC

NOTES
_____
_____
_____
_____
_____
_____
_____
_____
_____
_____
_____

KEY VERSES

PRAYER
_____
_____
_____
_____
_____
_____
_____

KEY POINTS

_____
_____
_____
_____
_____
_____
_____

APPLICATION

Prayer journal

DATE _____

PREACHER   SERMON TOPIC

NOTES
_____
_____
_____
_____
_____
_____
_____
_____
_____
_____
_____
_____
_____

KEY VERSES

PRAYER
_____
_____
_____
_____
_____
_____
_____
_____
_____
_____
_____
_____
_____
_____
_____
_____

KEY POINTS

APPLICATION

Prayer journal

DATE _____

TODAY'S PASSAGE

PREACHER

SERMON TOPIC

NOTES
_____
_____
_____
_____
_____
_____
_____
_____
_____
_____
_____

KEY VERSES

PRAYER
_____
_____
_____
_____
_____
_____
_____
_____
_____
_____
_____
_____
_____

KEY POINTS

APPLICATION

Prayer journal

DATE

TODAY'S PASSAGE

PREACHER

SERMON TOPIC

NOTES

KEY VERSES

PRAYER

KEY POINTS

APPLICATION

DATE _____

Prayer journal

TODAY'S PASSAGE

PREACHER

SERMON TOPIC

NOTES

KEY VERSES

PRAYER

KEY POINTS

APPLICATION

Prayer journal

DATE _____

TODAY'S PASSAGE | PREACHER | SERMON TOPIC

NOTES
_____
_____
_____
_____
_____
_____
_____
_____
_____
_____
_____
_____

KEY VERSES

PRAYER
_____
_____
_____
_____
_____
_____

KEY POINTS

_____
_____
_____
_____
_____
_____
_____
_____
_____

APPLICATION

Prayer journal

DATE _____

TODAY'S PASSAGE

PREACHER

SERMON TOPIC

NOTES

_____

_____

_____

_____

_____

_____

_____

_____

_____

_____

_____

KEY VERSES

PRAYER

_____

_____

_____

_____

_____

KEY POINTS

_____

_____

_____

_____

_____

_____

_____

APPLICATION

Prayer journal

DATE _____

TODAY'S PASSAGE _____ PREACHER _____ SERMON TOPIC _____

NOTES
_____
_____
_____
_____
_____
_____
_____
_____
_____
_____
_____
_____

KEY VERSES

PRAYER
_____
_____
_____
_____
_____
_____
_____
_____
_____
_____
_____
_____
_____
_____
_____
_____

KEY POINTS

APPLICATION

Prayer journal

DATE _____

TODAY'S PASSAGE

PREACHER

SERMON TOPIC

NOTES
_____
_____
_____
_____
_____
_____
_____
_____
_____
_____
_____
_____

KEY VERSES

PRAYER
_____
_____
_____
_____
_____
_____

KEY POINTS

_____
_____
_____
_____
_____
_____
_____
_____

APPLICATION

Prayer journal

DATE _____

TODAY'S PASSAGE | PREACHER | SERMON TOPIC

NOTES
_____
_____
_____
_____
_____
_____
_____
_____
_____
_____
_____
_____

KEY VERSES

PRAYER
_____
_____
_____
_____
_____
_____
_____
_____
_____
_____
_____
_____
_____
_____
_____

KEY POINTS

APPLICATION

DATE _____

Prayer journal

TODAY'S PASSAGE   PREACHER   SERMON TOPIC

NOTES
_____
_____
_____
_____
_____
_____
_____
_____
_____
_____
_____
_____

KEY VERSES

PRAYER
_____
_____
_____
_____
_____

KEY POINTS

_____
_____
_____
_____
_____
_____

APPLICATION

DATE _____

Prayer journal

NOTES
_____

KEY VERSES

PRAYER
_____

KEY POINTS

APPLICATION

DATE

Prayer journal

TODAY'S PASSAGE

PREACHER

SERMON TOPIC

NOTES

KEY VERSES

PRAYER

KEY POINTS

APPLICATION

Prayer journal

DATE _____

TODAY'S PASSAGE

PREACHER

SERMON TOPIC

NOTES
_____
_____
_____
_____
_____
_____
_____
_____
_____
_____
_____
_____
_____

KEY VERSES

PRAYER
_____
_____
_____
_____
_____
_____
_____
_____
_____
_____
_____
_____
_____
_____
_____
_____

KEY POINTS

APPLICATION

Prayer journal

DATE _____

TODAY'S PASSAGE

PREACHER

SERMON TOPIC

NOTES

_____
_____
_____
_____
_____
_____
_____
_____
_____
_____
_____
_____

KEY VERSES

PRAYER

_____
_____
_____
_____
_____

KEY POINTS

_____
_____
_____
_____
_____
_____
_____

APPLICATION

Prayer journal

DATE _____

TODAY'S PASSAGE

PREACHER

SERMON TOPIC

NOTES

_____

_____

_____

_____

_____

_____

_____

_____

_____

_____

_____

_____

_____

KEY VERSES

PRAYER

_____

_____

_____

_____

_____

_____

_____

_____

_____

_____

_____

_____

_____

_____

_____

_____

KEY POINTS

APPLICATION

Prayer journal

DATE _____

TODAY'S PASSAGE _____   PREACHER _____   SERMON TOPIC _____

NOTES
_____
_____
_____
_____
_____
_____
_____
_____
_____
_____
_____
_____

KEY VERSES

PRAYER
_____
_____
_____
_____
_____

KEY POINTS

_____
_____
_____
_____
_____
_____
_____
_____

APPLICATION

Prayer journal

DATE _____

TODAY'S PASSAGE | PREACHER | SERMON TOPIC

NOTES
_____
_____
_____
_____
_____
_____
_____
_____
_____
_____
_____

KEY VERSES

PRAYER
_____
_____
_____
_____
_____
_____
_____
_____
_____
_____
_____
_____
_____
_____
_____
_____

KEY POINTS

APPLICATION

Prayer journal

DATE _____

TODAY'S PASSAGE

PREACHER

SERMON TOPIC

NOTES
_____
_____
_____
_____
_____
_____
_____
_____
_____
_____

KEY VERSES

PRAYER
_____
_____
_____
_____
_____
_____
_____
_____
_____
_____
_____
_____
_____
_____

KEY POINTS

APPLICATION

Prayer journal

DATE _____

TODAY'S PASSAGE

PREACHER

SERMON TOPIC

NOTES
_____
_____
_____
_____
_____
_____
_____
_____
_____
_____
_____

KEY VERSES

KEY POINTS

PRAYER
_____
_____
_____
_____
_____
_____
_____
_____
_____
_____
_____
_____
_____

APPLICATION

Prayer journal

DATE _____

TODAY'S PASSAGE   PREACHER   SERMON TOPIC

NOTES
_____
_____
_____
_____
_____
_____
_____
_____
_____
_____
_____

KEY VERSES

PRAYER
_____
_____
_____
_____
_____
_____

KEY POINTS

_____
_____
_____
_____
_____
_____
_____
_____

APPLICATION

Prayer journal

DATE _____

TODAY'S PASSAGE

PREACHER

SERMON TOPIC

NOTES

_____
_____
_____
_____
_____
_____
_____
_____
_____
_____
_____
_____
_____

KEY VERSES

PRAYER

_____
_____
_____
_____
_____
_____
_____
_____
_____
_____
_____
_____
_____
_____
_____
_____
_____

KEY POINTS

APPLICATION

Prayer journal

DATE _____

TODAY'S PASSAGE | PREACHER | SERMON TOPIC

NOTES
_____
_____
_____
_____
_____
_____
_____
_____
_____
_____
_____
_____

KEY VERSES

PRAYER
_____
_____
_____
_____
_____
_____
_____
_____
_____
_____
_____
_____
_____
_____

KEY POINTS

APPLICATION

DATE _____

Prayer journal

TODAY'S PASSAGE   PREACHER   SERMON TOPIC

NOTES
_____
_____
_____
_____
_____
_____
_____
_____
_____
_____
_____
_____
_____
_____

PRAYER
_____
_____
_____
_____
_____
_____
_____
_____
_____
_____
_____
_____
_____
_____
_____
_____
_____

KEY VERSES

KEY POINTS

APPLICATION

Prayer journal

DATE _____

TODAY'S PASSAGE   PREACHER   SERMON TOPIC

NOTES
_____
_____
_____
_____
_____
_____
_____
_____
_____
_____
_____

KEY VERSES

PRAYER
_____
_____
_____
_____
_____

KEY POINTS

_____
_____
_____
_____
_____
_____
_____
_____

APPLICATION

DATE _____

Prayer journal

PREACHER SERMON TOPIC

NOTES
_____
_____
_____
_____
_____
_____
_____
_____
_____
_____
_____

KEY VERSES

PRAYER
_____
_____
_____
_____
_____
_____
_____
_____
_____
_____
_____
_____
_____
_____
_____

KEY POINTS

APPLICATION

Prayer journal

DATE _____

TODAY'S PASSAGE | PREACHER | SERMON TOPIC

NOTES

_____
_____
_____
_____
_____
_____
_____
_____
_____
_____
_____
_____

PRAYER

_____
_____
_____
_____
_____
_____
_____
_____
_____
_____
_____
_____
_____

KEY VERSES

KEY POINTS

APPLICATION

Prayer journal

DATE _____

| TODAY'S PASSAGE | PREACHER | SERMON TOPIC |

NOTES
_____
_____
_____
_____
_____
_____
_____
_____
_____
_____
_____
_____
_____
_____

PRAYER
_____
_____
_____
_____
_____
_____
_____
_____
_____
_____
_____
_____
_____
_____
_____
_____

KEY VERSES

KEY POINTS

APPLICATION

Prayer journal

DATE _____

TODAY'S PASSAGE | PREACHER | SERMON TOPIC

NOTES
_____
_____
_____
_____
_____
_____
_____
_____
_____
_____
_____

PRAYER
_____
_____
_____
_____
_____
_____
_____
_____
_____
_____
_____
_____
_____

KEY VERSES

KEY POINTS

APPLICATION

DATE _____

Prayer journal

TODAY'S PASSAGE | PREACHER | SERMON TOPIC

NOTES
_____
_____
_____
_____
_____
_____
_____
_____
_____
_____
_____

KEY VERSES

PRAYER
_____
_____
_____
_____
_____
_____

KEY POINTS

_____
_____
_____
_____
_____
_____
_____

APPLICATION

Prayer journal

DATE _____

TODAY'S PASSAGE

PREACHER

SERMON TOPIC

NOTES
_____
_____
_____
_____
_____
_____
_____
_____
_____
_____
_____

KEY VERSES

PRAYER
_____
_____
_____
_____
_____

KEY POINTS

_____
_____
_____
_____
_____
_____
_____
_____

APPLICATION

Prayer journal

DATE _____

| TODAY'S PASSAGE | PREACHER | SERMON TOPIC |

NOTES

_____
_____
_____
_____
_____
_____
_____
_____
_____
_____
_____

PRAYER

_____
_____
_____
_____
_____
_____
_____
_____
_____
_____
_____
_____
_____
_____

KEY VERSES

KEY POINTS

APPLICATION

DATE _____

Prayer journal

TODAY'S PASSAGE

PREACHER

SERMON TOPIC

NOTES
_____
_____
_____
_____
_____
_____
_____
_____
_____
_____
_____
_____

KEY VERSES

PRAYER
_____
_____
_____
_____
_____

KEY POINTS

_____
_____
_____
_____
_____
_____
_____
_____

APPLICATION

Prayer journal

DATE _____

| TODAY'S PASSAGE | PREACHER | SERMON TOPIC |

NOTES
_____
_____
_____
_____
_____
_____
_____
_____
_____
_____
_____
_____

KEY VERSES

PRAYER
_____
_____
_____
_____
_____
_____
_____
_____
_____
_____
_____
_____
_____
_____
_____
_____

KEY POINTS

APPLICATION

Prayer journal

DATE _____

TODAY'S PASSAGE   PREACHER   SERMON TOPIC

NOTES
_____
_____
_____
_____
_____
_____
_____
_____
_____
_____
_____

PRAYER
_____
_____
_____
_____
_____
_____
_____
_____
_____
_____
_____

KEY VERSES

KEY POINTS

APPLICATION

Prayer journal

DATE

TODAY'S PASSAGE

PREACHER

SERMON TOPIC

NOTES

KEY VERSES

PRAYER

KEY POINTS

APPLICATION

Prayer journal

DATE _____

TODAY'S PASSAGE   PREACHER   SERMON TOPIC

NOTES
_____
_____
_____
_____
_____
_____
_____
_____
_____
_____
_____

PRAYER
_____
_____
_____
_____
_____
_____
_____
_____
_____
_____
_____
_____

KEY VERSES

KEY POINTS

APPLICATION

Prayer journal

DATE _____

| TODAY'S PASSAGE | PREACHER | SERMON TOPIC |

NOTES
_____
_____
_____
_____
_____
_____
_____
_____
_____
_____
_____
_____

PRAYER
_____
_____
_____
_____
_____
_____
_____
_____
_____
_____
_____
_____
_____
_____
_____
_____
_____

KEY VERSES

KEY POINTS

APPLICATION

Prayer journal

DATE _____

TODAY'S PASSAGE

PREACHER

SERMON TOPIC

NOTES

_____
_____
_____
_____
_____
_____
_____
_____
_____
_____
_____
_____

PRAYER

_____
_____
_____
_____
_____
_____
_____
_____
_____
_____
_____
_____

KEY VERSES

KEY POINTS

APPLICATION

Prayer journal

DATE _____

TODAY'S PASSAGE   PREACHER   SERMON TOPIC

NOTES
_____
_____
_____
_____
_____
_____
_____
_____
_____
_____
_____
_____
_____

KEY VERSES

PRAYER
_____
_____
_____
_____
_____
_____
_____
_____
_____
_____
_____
_____
_____
_____
_____

KEY POINTS

APPLICATION

Prayer journal

DATE _____

TODAY'S PASSAGE

PREACHER

SERMON TOPIC

NOTES

_____
_____
_____
_____
_____
_____
_____
_____
_____
_____
_____
_____

PRAYER

_____
_____
_____
_____
_____
_____
_____
_____
_____
_____
_____
_____
_____

KEY VERSES

KEY POINTS

APPLICATION

Prayer journal

DATE _____

TODAY'S PASSAGE

PREACHER

SERMON TOPIC

NOTES

_____
_____
_____
_____
_____
_____
_____
_____
_____
_____
_____

KEY VERSES

PRAYER

_____
_____
_____
_____
_____
_____
_____
_____
_____
_____
_____
_____
_____
_____
_____

KEY POINTS

APPLICATION

Prayer journal

DATE _____

NOTES
_____
_____
_____
_____
_____
_____
_____
_____
_____
_____
_____
_____
_____

PRAYER
_____
_____
_____
_____
_____
_____
_____
_____
_____
_____
_____
_____
_____
_____
_____

KEY VERSES

KEY POINTS

APPLICATION

Prayer journal

DATE _____

TODAY'S PASSAGE | PREACHER | SERMON TOPIC

NOTES
_____
_____
_____
_____
_____
_____
_____
_____
_____
_____
_____

KEY VERSES

PRAYER
_____
_____
_____
_____
_____

KEY POINTS

_____
_____
_____
_____
_____
_____
_____

APPLICATION

Prayer journal

DATE _____

TODAY'S PASSAGE   PREACHER   SERMON TOPIC

NOTES
_____
_____
_____
_____
_____
_____
_____
_____
_____
_____
_____
_____

KEY VERSES

PRAYER
_____
_____
_____
_____
_____
_____
_____
_____
_____
_____
_____
_____
_____
_____
_____
_____

KEY POINTS

APPLICATION

Prayer journal

DATE _____

TODAY'S PASSAGE | PREACHER | SERMON TOPIC

NOTES

KEY VERSES

PRAYER

KEY POINTS

APPLICATION

DATE _____

Prayer journal

TODAY'S PASSAGE

PREACHER

SERMON TOPIC

NOTES
_____

KEY VERSES

PRAYER
_____

KEY POINTS

APPLICATION

DATE _____

Prayer journal

TODAY'S PASSAGE   PREACHER   SERMON TOPIC

NOTES
_____
_____
_____
_____
_____
_____
_____
_____
_____
_____
_____

KEY VERSES

PRAYER
_____
_____
_____
_____
_____

KEY POINTS

_____
_____
_____
_____
_____
_____
_____
_____
_____

APPLICATION

DATE _____

Prayer journal

TODAY'S PASSAGE   PREACHER   SERMON TOPIC

NOTES

_____
_____
_____
_____
_____
_____
_____
_____
_____
_____
_____
_____
_____

PRAYER

_____
_____
_____
_____
_____
_____
_____
_____
_____
_____
_____
_____
_____
_____
_____
_____
_____

KEY VERSES

KEY POINTS

APPLICATION

Prayer journal

DATE _____

TODAY'S PASSAGE

PREACHER

SERMON TOPIC

NOTES
_____
_____
_____
_____
_____
_____
_____
_____
_____
_____
_____
_____

KEY VERSES

PRAYER
_____
_____
_____
_____
_____
_____
_____
_____
_____
_____
_____
_____

KEY POINTS

APPLICATION

Prayer journal

DATE _____

PREACHER   SERMON TOPIC

NOTES
_____
_____
_____
_____
_____
_____
_____
_____
_____
_____
_____
_____

KEY VERSES

PRAYER
_____
_____
_____
_____
_____
_____
_____

KEY POINTS

_____
_____
_____
_____
_____
_____
_____
_____
_____
_____

APPLICATION

Prayer journal

DATE _____

TODAY'S PASSAGE	PREACHER	SERMON TOPIC

NOTES
_____
_____
_____
_____
_____
_____
_____
_____
_____
_____
_____

KEY VERSES

PRAYER
_____
_____
_____
_____
_____

KEY POINTS

_____
_____
_____
_____
_____
_____
_____

APPLICATION

Prayer journal

DATE _____

TODAY'S PASSAGE

PREACHER

SERMON TOPIC

NOTES
_____
_____
_____
_____
_____
_____
_____
_____
_____
_____
_____
_____
_____
_____

KEY VERSES

PRAYER
_____
_____
_____
_____
_____
_____
_____
_____
_____
_____
_____
_____
_____
_____
_____
_____
_____
_____
_____

KEY POINTS

APPLICATION

Prayer journal

DATE _____

TODAY'S PASSAGE

PREACHER

SERMON TOPIC

NOTES

KEY VERSES

PRAYER

KEY POINTS

APPLICATION

DATE _____

Prayer journal

PREACHER   SERMON TOPIC

NOTES
_____
_____
_____
_____
_____
_____
_____
_____
_____
_____
_____
_____
_____

KEY VERSES

PRAYER
_____
_____
_____
_____
_____
_____
_____
_____

KEY POINTS

_____
_____
_____
_____
_____
_____
_____
_____

APPLICATION

Prayer journal

DATE _____

TODAY'S PASSAGE | PREACHER | SERMON TOPIC

NOTES

_____

_____

_____

_____

_____

_____

_____

_____

_____

_____

KEY VERSES

PRAYER

_____

_____

_____

_____

_____

_____

_____

_____

_____

_____

_____

_____

_____

_____

KEY POINTS

APPLICATION

DATE _____

Prayer journal

NOTES
_____
_____
_____
_____
_____
_____
_____
_____
_____
_____
_____
_____
_____

KEY VERSES

PRAYER
_____
_____
_____
_____
_____
_____
_____
_____

KEY POINTS

_____
_____
_____
_____
_____
_____
_____
_____
_____
_____

APPLICATION

Prayer journal

DATE _____

NOTES
_____
_____
_____
_____
_____
_____
_____
_____
_____
_____

KEY VERSES

PRAYER
_____
_____
_____
_____
_____
_____
_____
_____
_____
_____
_____
_____
_____

KEY POINTS

APPLICATION

DATE _____

Prayer journal

TODAY'S PASSAGE   PREACHER   SERMON TOPIC

NOTES
_____
_____
_____
_____
_____
_____
_____
_____
_____
_____
_____
_____

KEY VERSES

PRAYER
_____
_____
_____
_____
_____
_____

KEY POINTS

_____
_____
_____
_____
_____
_____
_____
_____
_____

APPLICATION

Prayer journal

DATE _____

PREACHER   SERMON TOPIC

NOTES
_____
_____
_____
_____
_____
_____
_____
_____
_____
_____
_____
_____

KEY VERSES

PRAYER
_____
_____
_____
_____
_____

KEY POINTS

_____
_____
_____
_____
_____
_____
_____

APPLICATION

DATE _____

Prayer journal

PREACHER SERMON TOPIC

NOTES
_____
_____
_____
_____
_____
_____
_____
_____
_____
_____
_____
_____
_____

KEY VERSES

PRAYER
_____
_____
_____
_____
_____
_____
_____
_____

KEY POINTS

_____
_____
_____
_____
_____
_____
_____
_____
_____

APPLICATION

Prayer journal

DATE _____

| TODAY'S PASSAGE | PREACHER | SERMON TOPIC |

NOTES
_____
_____
_____
_____
_____
_____
_____
_____
_____
_____
_____
_____

KEY VERSES

PRAYER
_____
_____
_____
_____
_____
_____
_____
_____
_____
_____
_____
_____
_____
_____

KEY POINTS

APPLICATION

DATE _____

Prayer journal

TODAY'S PASSAGE   PREACHER   SERMON TOPIC

NOTES
_____
_____   KEY VERSES
_____
_____
_____
_____
_____
_____
_____
_____
_____
_____
_____
_____
_____   KEY POINTS
_____

PRAYER
_____
_____
_____
_____
_____
_____
_____
_____   APPLICATION
_____
_____
_____
_____
_____
_____
_____
_____
_____

Prayer journal

DATE _____

TODAY'S PASSAGE | PREACHER | SERMON TOPIC

NOTES
_____
_____
_____
_____
_____
_____
_____
_____
_____
_____
_____

KEY VERSES

PRAYER
_____
_____
_____
_____
_____

KEY POINTS

_____
_____
_____
_____
_____
_____
_____
_____

APPLICATION

DATE

Prayer journal

NOTES

KEY VERSES

PRAYER

KEY POINTS

APPLICATION

DATE _____

Prayer journal

TODAY'S PASSAGE   PREACHER   SERMON TOPIC

NOTES
_____
_____
_____
_____   KEY VERSES
_____
_____
_____
_____
_____
_____
_____
_____

_____   KEY POINTS

PRAYER
_____
_____
_____
_____
_____
_____

_____   APPLICATION
_____
_____
_____
_____
_____
_____
_____
_____

DATE _____

Prayer journal

TODAY'S PASSAGE   PREACHER   SERMON TOPIC

NOTES
_____
_____
_____
_____
_____
_____
_____
_____
_____
_____
_____
_____
_____

KEY VERSES

PRAYER
_____
_____
_____
_____
_____
_____
_____
_____

KEY POINTS

_____
_____
_____
_____
_____
_____
_____
_____
_____

APPLICATION

Prayer journal

DATE

TODAY'S PASSAGE

PREACHER

SERMON TOPIC

NOTES

KEY VERSES

PRAYER

KEY POINTS

APPLICATION

DATE _____

Prayer journal

TODAY'S PASSAGE   PREACHER   SERMON TOPIC

NOTES
_____
_____
_____
_____
_____
_____
_____
_____
_____
_____
_____
_____

KEY VERSES

PRAYER
_____
_____
_____
_____
_____
_____

KEY POINTS

_____
_____
_____
_____
_____
_____
_____
_____

APPLICATION

Prayer journal

DATE _____

| TODAY'S PASSAGE | PREACHER | SERMON TOPIC |

NOTES
_____
_____
_____
_____
_____
_____
_____
_____
_____
_____
_____

KEY VERSES

PRAYER
_____
_____
_____
_____
_____
_____
_____
_____
_____
_____
_____
_____

KEY POINTS

APPLICATION

Prayer journal

DATE _____

TODAY'S PASSAGE   PREACHER   SERMON TOPIC

NOTES
_____
_____
_____
_____
_____
_____
_____
_____
_____
_____
_____
_____

PRAYER
_____
_____
_____
_____
_____
_____
_____
_____
_____
_____
_____
_____
_____
_____
_____
_____

KEY VERSES

KEY POINTS

APPLICATION

Prayer journal

DATE _____

TODAY'S PASSAGE

PREACHER

SERMON TOPIC

NOTES
_____
_____
_____
_____
_____
_____
_____
_____
_____
_____
_____
_____

KEY VERSES

PRAYER
_____
_____
_____
_____
_____

KEY POINTS

_____
_____
_____
_____
_____
_____
_____
_____
_____

APPLICATION

DATE _____

Prayer journal

PREACHER SERMON TOPIC

NOTES
_____
_____
_____
_____
_____
_____
_____
_____
_____
_____
_____
_____
_____
_____
_____
_____

KEY VERSES

PRAYER
_____
_____
_____
_____
_____
_____
_____
_____
_____
_____
_____
_____
_____
_____
_____
_____
_____
_____

KEY POINTS

APPLICATION

Prayer journal

DATE _____

TODAY'S PASSAGE   PREACHER   SERMON TOPIC

NOTES
_____
_____
_____
_____
_____
_____
_____
_____
_____
_____
_____

KEY VERSES

PRAYER
_____
_____
_____
_____
_____
_____
_____
_____
_____
_____
_____
_____
_____

KEY POINTS

APPLICATION

DATE _____

Prayer journal

TODAY'S PASSAGE   PREACHER   SERMON TOPIC

NOTES
_____
_____
_____
_____
_____
_____
_____
_____
_____
_____
_____
_____
_____
_____

KEY VERSES

PRAYER
_____
_____
_____
_____
_____
_____
_____

KEY POINTS

_____
_____
_____
_____
_____
_____
_____
_____

APPLICATION

Prayer journal

DATE _____

| TODAY'S PASSAGE | PREACHER | SERMON TOPIC |

NOTES
_____
_____
_____
_____
_____
_____
_____
_____
_____
_____
_____
_____

KEY VERSES

PRAYER
_____
_____
_____
_____
_____
_____

KEY POINTS

_____
_____
_____
_____
_____
_____
_____
_____

APPLICATION

DATE _____

Prayer journal

TODAY'S PASSAGE   PREACHER   SERMON TOPIC

NOTES
_____
_____
_____
_____
_____
_____
_____
_____
_____
_____
_____
_____
_____

KEY VERSES

PRAYER
_____
_____
_____
_____
_____
_____
_____
_____

KEY POINTS

_____
_____
_____
_____
_____
_____
_____
_____
_____
_____

APPLICATION

Prayer journal

DATE _____

TODAY'S PASSAGE

PREACHER

SERMON TOPIC

NOTES
_____
_____
_____
_____
_____
_____
_____
_____
_____
_____
_____
_____

KEY VERSES

PRAYER
_____
_____
_____
_____
_____
_____
_____
_____
_____
_____
_____
_____
_____
_____

KEY POINTS

APPLICATION

DATE _____

Prayer journal

    PREACHER   SERMON TOPIC

NOTES
_____
_____
_____
_____
_____
_____
_____
_____
_____
_____
_____
_____
_____
_____

KEY VERSES

PRAYER
_____
_____
_____
_____
_____
_____
_____

KEY POINTS

_____
_____
_____
_____
_____
_____
_____
_____
_____
_____
_____

APPLICATION

Prayer journal

DATE _____

TODAY'S PASSAGE

PREACHER

SERMON TOPIC

NOTES
_____
_____
_____
_____
_____
_____
_____
_____
_____
_____

KEY VERSES

PRAYER
_____
_____
_____
_____
_____
_____
_____

KEY POINTS

_____
_____
_____
_____
_____
_____
_____
_____

APPLICATION

Prayer journal

DATE _____

TODAY'S PASSAGE   PREACHER   SERMON TOPIC

NOTES
_____
_____
_____
_____
_____
_____
_____
_____
_____
_____
_____
_____

KEY VERSES

PRAYER
_____
_____
_____
_____
_____
_____
_____
_____

KEY POINTS

_____
_____
_____
_____
_____
_____
_____
_____

APPLICATION

Prayer journal

DATE

TODAY'S PASSAGE

PREACHER

SERMON TOPIC

NOTES

KEY VERSES

PRAYER

KEY POINTS

APPLICATION

Prayer journal

DATE _____

TODAY'S PASSAGE _____   PREACHER _____   SERMON TOPIC _____

NOTES
_____
_____
_____
_____
_____
_____
_____
_____
_____
_____
_____
_____

PRAYER
_____
_____
_____
_____
_____
_____
_____
_____
_____
_____
_____
_____
_____
_____
_____
_____
_____
_____

KEY VERSES

KEY POINTS

APPLICATION

Prayer journal

DATE

TODAY'S PASSAGE

PREACHER

SERMON TOPIC

NOTES

KEY VERSES

PRAYER

KEY POINTS

APPLICATION

Prayer journal

DATE _____

TODAY'S PASSAGE | PREACHER | SERMON TOPIC

NOTES
_____
_____
_____
_____
_____
_____
_____
_____
_____
_____
_____
_____
_____
_____

KEY VERSES

PRAYER
_____
_____
_____
_____
_____
_____
_____
_____
_____
_____
_____
_____
_____
_____
_____
_____
_____
_____

KEY POINTS

APPLICATION

Prayer journal

DATE

TODAY'S PASSAGE

PREACHER

SERMON TOPIC

NOTES

KEY VERSES

PRAYER

KEY POINTS

APPLICATION

DATE _____

Prayer journal

NOTES
_____

_____

_____

_____

_____

_____

_____

_____

_____

_____

_____

_____

KEY VERSES

PRAYER
_____

_____

_____

_____

_____

_____

_____

KEY POINTS

_____

_____

_____

_____

_____

_____

_____

_____

_____

APPLICATION

DATE _____

Prayer journal

TODAY'S PASSAGE   PREACHER   SERMON TOPIC

NOTES
_____
_____
_____
_____
_____
_____
_____
_____
_____
_____
_____
_____

PRAYER
_____
_____
_____
_____
_____
_____
_____
_____
_____
_____
_____
_____

KEY VERSES

KEY POINTS

APPLICATION

DATE _____

Prayer journal

TODAY'S PASSAGE   PREACHER   SERMON TOPIC

NOTES
_____

KEY VERSES

_____

KEY POINTS

PRAYER
_____

APPLICATION

Prayer journal

DATE _____

TODAY'S PASSAGE | PREACHER | SERMON TOPIC

NOTES
_____
_____
_____
_____
_____
_____
_____
_____
_____
_____
_____
_____
_____

KEY VERSES

PRAYER
_____
_____
_____
_____
_____
_____

KEY POINTS

_____
_____
_____
_____
_____
_____
_____
_____
_____
_____

APPLICATION

Made in the USA
Coppell, TX
18 December 2023

26545943R10060